THE BACCHAE

EURIPIDES
THE BACCHAE

Translated into English rhyming verse
with Explanatory Notes

by
GILBERT MURRAY

London
GEORGE ALLEN & UNWIN LTD
Museum Street

First Edition						November	1904
Second Impression						September	1910
Third	„	.	.	.	.	August	1913
Fourth	„	.	.	.	.	July	1916
Fifth	„	.	.	.	.	March	1919
Sixth	„	.	.	.	.	November	1920
Seventh	„	.	.	.	.	December	1924
Eighth	„	.	.	.	.	July	1927
Ninth	„	.	.	.	.	November	1931
Tenth	„	.	.	.	.	November	1937
Eleventh	„	.	.	.	.	January	1941
Twelfth	„	.	.	.	.		1946
Thirteenth	„	.	.	.	.		1948
Fourteenth	„	.	.	.	.		1957
Fifteenth	„	.	.	.	.		1961
Sixteenth	„	.	.	.	.		1971
Seventeenth	„	.	.	.	.		1975

ISBN 0 04 882030 X

Distributed in the United States of America
by Oxford University Press, Inc.

Printed in Great Britain by
Lewis Reprints Limited, London and Tonbridge

CHARACTERS IN THE PLAY

DIONŶSUS, THE GOD : *son of Zeus and of the Theban princess Semelê.*

CADMUS, *formerly King of Thebes, father of Semelê.*

PENTHEUS, *King of Thebes, son of Echîon, grandson of Cadmus.*

AGÂVÈ, *daughter of Cadmus, mother of Pentheus.*

TEIRESIAS, *an aged Theban prophet.*

A SOLDIER OF PENTHEUS' GUARD.

TWO MESSENGERS.

A CHORUS OF INSPIRED DAMSELS, *following Dionysus from the East.*

"The play was first produced after the death of Euripides by his son, who bore the same name, together with the 'Iphigenîa in Aulis' and the 'Alcmaeon,' probably in the year 405 B.C."

THE BACCHAE

The background represents the front of the Castle of PENTHEUS,
  *King of Thebes.   At one side is visible the sacred Tomb of
  Semelê, a little enclosure overgrown with wild vines, with
  a cleft in the rocky floor of it from which there issues at times
  steam or smoke.   The God* DIONYSUS *is discovered alone.*

DIONYSUS

Behold, God's Son is come unto this land
Of Thebes, even I, Dionysus, whom the brand
Of heaven's hot splendour lit to life, when she
Who bore me, Cadmus' daughter Semelê,
Died here.   So, changed in shape from God to man,
I walk again by Dircê's streams and scan
Ismênus' shore.   There by the castle side
I see her place, the Tomb of the Lightning's Bride,

7

The wreck of smouldering chambers, and the great
Faint wreaths of fire undying—as the hate
Dies not, that Hera held for Semelê.

Aye, Cadmus hath done well; in purity
He keeps this place apart, inviolate,
His daughter's sanctuary; and I have set
My green and clustered vines to robe it round.

Far now behind me lies the golden ground
Of Lydian and of Phrygian; far away
The wide hot plains where Persian sunbeams play,
The Bactrian war-holds, and the storm-oppressed
Clime of the Mede, and Araby the Blest,
And Asia all, that by the salt sea lies
In proud embattled cities, motley-wise
Of Hellene and Barbarian interwrought;
And now I come to Hellas—having taught
All the world else my dances and my rite
Of mysteries, to show me in men's sight
Manifest God.

And first of Hellene lands
I cry this Thebes to waken; set her hands
To clasp my wand, mine ivied javelin,
And round her shoulders hang my wild fawn-skin.
For they have scorned me whom it least beseemed,
Semelê's sisters; mocked my birth, nor deemed
That Dionysus sprang from Dian seed.
My mother sinned, said they; and in her need,
With Cadmus plotting, cloaked her human shame
With the dread name of Zeus; for that the flame
From heaven consumed her, seeing she lied to God.

Thus must they vaunt; and therefore hath my rod
On them first fallen, and stung them forth wild-eyed
From empty chambers; the bare mountain side
Is made their home, and all their hearts are flame.

Yea, I have bound upon the necks of them
The harness of my rites.   And with them all
The seed of womankind from hut and hall
Of Thebes, hath this my magic goaded out.
And there, with the old King's daughters, in a rout
Confused, they make their dwelling-place between
The roofless rocks and shadowy pine trees green.
Thus shall this Thebes, how sore soe'er it smart,
Learn and forget not, till she crave her part
In mine adoring; thus must I speak clear
To save my mother's fame, and crown me here
As true God, born by Semelê to Zeus.

Now Cadmus yieldeth up his throne and use
Of royal honour to his daughter's son
Pentheus; who on my body hath begun
A war with God.   He thrusteth me away
From due drink-offering, and, when men pray,
My name entreats not.   Therefore on his own
Head and his people's shall my power be shown.
Then to another land, when all things here
Are well, must I fare onward, making clear
My godhead's might.   But should this Theban town
Essay with wrath and battle to drag down
My maids, lo, in their path myself shall be,
And maniac armies battled after me!
For this I veil my godhead with the wan
Form of the things that die, and walk as Man.

O Brood of Tmolus o'er the wide world flown,
O Lydian band, my chosen and mine own,
Damsels uplifted o'er the orient deep
To wander where I wander, and to sleep
Where I sleep; up, and wake the old sweet sound,
The clang that I and mystic Rhea found,

The Timbrel of the Mountain! Gather all
Thebes to your song round Pentheus' royal hall.
I seek my new-made worshippers, to guide
Their dances up Kithaeron's pine-clad side.

[*As he departs, there comes stealing in from the left a band of
fifteen Eastern Women, the light of the sunrise streaming
upon their long white robes and ivy-bound hair. They wear
fawn-skins over the robes, and carry some of them timbrels,
some pipes and other instruments. Many bear the thyrsus,
or sacred Wand, made of reed ringed with ivy. They enter
stealthily till they see that the place is empty, and then begin
their mystic song of worship.*

CHORUS

A Maiden

From Asia, from the dayspring that uprises,
　　To Bromios ever glorying we came.
We laboured for our Lord in many guises;
We toiled, but the toil is as the prize is;
　　Thou Mystery, we hail thee by thy name!

Another

Who lingers in the road? Who espies us?
　　He shall hide him in his house nor be bold.
Let the heart keep silence that defies us;
For I sing this day to Dionysus
　　The song that is appointed from of old.

All the Maidens

Oh, blessèd he in all wise,
　　Who hath drunk the Living Fountain,
　　　　Whose life no folly staineth,
　　　　　　And his soul is near to God;

Whose sins are lifted, pall-wise,
  As he worships on the Mountain,
    And where Cybele ordaineth,
    Our Mother, he has trod:

    His head with ivy laden
      And his thyrsus tossing high,
      For our God he lifts his cry;
    " Up, O Bacchae, wife and maiden,
        Come, O ye Bacchae, come;
    Oh, bring the Joy-bestower,
    God-seed of God the Sower,
    Bring Bromios in his power
        From Phrygia's mountain dome;
    To street and town and tower,
        Oh, bring ye Bromios home!"

Whom erst in anguish lying
  For an unborn life's desire,
    As a dead thing in the Thunder
    His mother cast to earth;
For her heart was dying, dying,
  In the white heart of the fire;
    Till Zeus, the Lord of Wonder,
    Devised new lairs of birth;

    Yea, his own flesh tore to hide him,
      And with clasps of bitter gold
      Did a secret son enfold,
    And the Queen knew not beside him;
      Till the perfect hour was there;
    Then a hornèd God was found,
    And a God with serpents crowned;

And for that are serpents wound
In the wands his maidens bear,
And the songs of serpents sound
In the mazes of their hair.

Some Maidens

All hail, O Thebes, thou nurse of Semelê!
With Semelê's wild ivy crown thy towers;
Oh, burst in bloom of wreathing bryony,
Berries and leaves and flowers;
Uplift the dark divine wand,
The oak-wand and the pine-wand,
And don thy fawn-skin, fringed in purity
With fleecy white, like ours.

Oh, cleanse thee in the wands' waving pride!
Yea, all men shall dance with us and pray,
When Bromios his companies shall guide
Hillward, ever hillward, where they stay,
The flock of the Believing,
The maids from loom and weaving
By the magic of his breath borne away.

Others

Hail thou, O Nurse of Zeus, O Caverned Haunt
Where fierce arms clanged to guard God's cradle
rare,
For thee of old some crested Corybant
First woke in Cretan air
The wild orb of our orgies,
Our Timbrel; and thy gorges
Rang with this strain; and blended Phrygian chant
And sweet keen pipes were there.

But the Timbrel, the Timbrel was another's,
   And away to Mother Rhea it must wend;
And to our holy singing from the Mother's
    The mad Satyrs carried it, to blend
      In the dancing and the cheer
      Of our third and perfect Year;
And it serves Dionysus in the end!

A Maiden

O glad, glad on the mountains
   To swoon in the race outworn,
     When the holy fawn-skin clings,
     And all else sweeps away,
To the joy of the red quick fountains,
   The blood of the hill-goat torn,
     The glory of wild-beast ravenings,
      Where the hill-tops catch the day;
To the Phrygian, Lydian, mountains!
   'Tis Bromios leads the way.

Another Maiden

Then streams the earth with milk, yea, streams
With wine and nectar of the bee,
And through the air dim perfume steams
Of Syrian frankincense; and He,
Our leader, from his thyrsus spray
A torchlight tosses high and higher,
A torchlight like a beacon-fire,
To waken all that faint and stray;
   And sets them leaping as he sings,
   His tresses rippling to the sky,
   And deep beneath the Maenad cry
     His proud voice rings:
       " Come, O ye Bacchae, come! "

All the Maidens

Hither, O fragrant of Tmolus the Golden,
   Come with the voice of timbrel and drum;
Let the cry of your joyance uplift and embolden
   The God of the joy-cry; O Bacchanals, come!
With pealing of pipes and with Phrygian clamour,
   On, where the vision of holiness thrills,
And the music climbs and the maddening glamour,
   With the wild White Maids, to the hills, to the hills!
Oh, then, like a colt as he runs by a river,
   A colt by his dam, when the heart of him sings,
With the keen limbs drawn and the fleet foot a-quiver,
      Away the Bacchanal springs!

[*Enter* TEIRESIAS. *He is an old man and blind, leaning upon
a staff and moving with slow stateliness, though wearing the
Ivy and the Bacchic fawn-skin.*

TEIRESIAS

Ho, there, who keeps the gate?—Go, summon me
Cadmus, Agênor's son, who crossed the sea
From Sidon and upreared this Theban hold.
Go, whosoe'er thou art. See he be told
Teiresias seeketh him. Himself will gauge
Mine errand, and the compact, age with age,
I vowed with him, grey hair with snow-white hair,
To deck the new God's thyrsus, and to wear
His fawn-skin, and with ivy crown our brows.

[*Enter* CADMUS *from the Castle. He is even older than*
TEIRESIAS, *and wears the same attire.*

CADMUS

True friend! I knew that voice of thine that flows
Like mellow wisdom from a fountain wise.
And, lo, I come prepared, in all the guise

14

And harness of this God.   Are we not told
His is the soul of that dead life of old
That sprang from mine own daughter?   Surely then
Must thou and I with all the strength of men
Exalt him.

    Where then shall I stand, where tread
The dance and toss this bowed and hoary head?
O friend, in thee is wisdom; guide my grey
And eld-worn steps, eld-worn Teiresias.—Nay;
I am not weak.

*[At the first movement of worship his manner begins to change;
 a mysterious strength and exaltation enter him.*
    Surely this arm could smite
The wild earth with its thyrsus, day and night,
And faint not!   Sweetly and forgetfully
The dim years fall from off me!

TEIRESIAS

     As with thee,
With me 'tis likewise.   Light am I and young,
And will essay the dancing and the song.

CADMUS

Quick, then, our chariots to the mountain road.

TEIRESIAS

Nay; to take steeds were to mistrust the God.

CADMUS

So be it.   Mine old arm shall guide thee there.

TEIRESIAS

The God himself shall guide!   Have thou no care.

CADMUS

And in all Thebes shall no man dance but we?

TEIRESIAS

Aye, Thebes is blinded.   Thou and I can see.

CADMUS

'Tis weary waiting; hold my hand, friend; so.

TEIRESIAS

Lo, there is mine.   So linkèd let us go.

CADMUS

Shall things of dust the Gods' dark ways despise?

TEIRESIAS

Or prove our wit on Heaven's high mysteries?
Not thou and I!   That heritage sublime
Our sires have left us, wisdom old as time,
No word of man, how deep soe'er his thought
And won of subtlest toil, may bring to naught.

Aye, men will rail that I forget my years.
To dance and wreathe with ivy these white hairs;
What recks it?   Seeing the God no line hath told
To mark what man shall dance, or young or old;
But craves his honours from mortality
All, no man marked apart; and great shall be!

CADMUS (*after looking away toward the Mountain*)
Teiresias, since this light thou canst not read,
I must be seer for thee.   Here comes in speed
Pentheus, Echîon's son, whom I have raised
To rule my people in my stead.—Amazed
He seems.   Stand close, and mark what we shall hear.

[The two stand back, partially concealed, while there enters in hot haste PENTHEUS, *followed by a bodyguard. He is speaking to the* SOLDIER *in command.*

PENTHEUS

Scarce had I crossed our borders, when mine ear
Was caught by this strange rumour, that our own
Wives, our own sisters, from their hearths are flown
To wild and secret rites; and cluster there
High on the shadowy hills, with dance and prayer
To adore this new-made God, this Dionyse,
Whate'er he be!—And in their companies
Deep wine-jars stand, and ever and anon
Away into the loneliness now one
Steals forth, and now a second, maid or dame,
Where love lies waiting, not of God!   The flame,
They say, of Bacchios wraps them.   Bacchios!   Nay,
'Tis more to Aphrodite that they pray.

  Howbeit, all that I have found, my men
Hold bound and shackled in our dungeon den;
The rest, I will go hunt them!   Aye, and snare
My birds with nets of iron, to quell their prayer
And mountain song and rites of rascaldom!

  They tell me, too, there is a stranger come,
A man of charm and spell, from Lydian seas,
A head all gold and cloudy fragrancies,
A wine-red cheek, and eyes that hold the light
Of the very Cyprian.   Day and livelong night
He haunts amid the damsels, o'er each lip
Dangling his cup of joyance!—Let me grip
Him once, but once, within these walls, right swift
That wand shall cease its music, and that drift
Of tossing curls lie still—when my rude sword
Falls between neck and trunk!   'Tis all his word,

B   17

This tale of Dionysus; how that same
Babe that was blasted by the lightning flame
With his dead mother, for that mother's lie,
Was re-conceived, born perfect from the thigh
Of Zeus, and now is God! What call ye these?
Dreams? Gibes of the unknown wanderer? Blasphemies
That crave the very gibbet?

              Stay! God wot,
Here is another marvel! See I not
In motley fawn-skins robed the vision-seer
Teiresias? And my mother's father here—
O depth of scorn!—adoring with the wand
Of Bacchios?—Father!—Nay, mine eyes are fond;
It is not your white heads so fancy-flown!
It cannot be! Cast off that ivy crown,
O mine own mother's sire! Set free that hand
That cowers about its staff.

              'Tis thou hast planned
This work, Teiresias! 'Tis thou must set
Another altar and another yet
Amongst us, watch new birds, and win more hire
Of gold, interpreting new signs of fire!
But for thy silver hairs, I tell thee true,
Thou now wert sitting chained amid thy crew
Of raving damsels, for this evil dream
Thou hast brought us, of new Gods! When once the gleam
Of grapes hath lit a Woman's Festival,
In all their prayers is no more health at all!

       LEADER OF THE CHORUS
     (the words are not heard by PENTHEUS)
Injurious King, hast thou no care for God,
Nor Cadmus, sower of the Giants' Sod,
Life-spring to great Echîon and to thee?

TEIRESIAS

Good words, my son, come easily, when he
That speaks is wise, and speaks but for the right.
Else come they never! Swift are thine, and bright
As though with thought, yet have no thought at all.

　　Lo, this new God, whom thou dost flout withal,
I cannot speak the greatness wherewith He
In Hellas shall be great! Two spirits there be,
Young Prince, that in man's world are first of worth.
Dêmêtêr one is named; she is the Earth—
Call her which name thou will!—who feeds man's frame
With sustenance of things dry. And that which came
Her work to perfect, second, is the Power
From Semelê born. He found the liquid shower
Hid in the grape. He rests man's spirit dim
From grieving, when the vine exalteth him.
He giveth sleep to sink the fretful day
In cool forgetting. Is there any way
With man's sore heart, save only to forget?

　　Yea, being God, the blood of him is set
Before the Gods in sacrifice, that we
For his sake may be blest.—And so, to thee,
That fable shames him, how this God was knit
Into God's flesh? Nay, learn the truth of it,
Cleared from the false.—When from that deadly light
Zeus saved the babe, and up to Olympus' height
Raised him, and Hera's wrath would cast him thence,
Then Zeus devised him a divine defence.
A fragment of the world-encircling fire
He rent apart, and wrought to his desire
Of shape and hue, in the image of the child,
And gave to Hera's rage. And so, beguiled
By change and passing time, this tale was born,
How the babe-god was hidden in the torn

19

Flesh of his sire.   He hath no shame thereby.

A prophet is he likewise.   Prophecy
Cleaves to all frenzy, but beyond all else
To frenzy of prayer.   Then in us verily dwells
The God himself, and speaks the thing to be.
Yea, and of Ares' realm a part hath he.
When mortal armies, mailèd and arrayed,
Have in strange fear, or ever blade met blade,
Fled maddened, 'tis this God hath palsied them.
Aye, over Delphi's rock-built diadem
Thou yet shalt see him leaping with his train
Of fire across the twin-peaked mountain-plain,
Flaming the darkness with his mystic wand,
And great in Hellas.—List and understand,
King Pentheus!   Dream not thou that force is power;
Nor, if thou hast a thought, and that thought sour
And sick, oh, dream not thought is wisdom!—Up,
Receive this God to Thebes; pour forth the cup
Of sacrifice, and pray, and wreathe thy brow.

Thou fearest for the damsels?   Think thee now;
How toucheth this the part of Dionyse
To hold maids pure perforce?   In them it lies,
And their own hearts; and in the wildest rite
Cometh no stain to her whose heart is white.

Nay, mark me!   Thou hast thy joy, when the Gate
Stands thronged, and Pentheus' name is lifted great
And high by Thebes in clamour; shall not He
Rejoice in his due meed of majesty?

Howbeit, this Cadmus whom thou scorn'st and I
Will wear His crown, and tread His dances!   Aye,
Our hairs are white, yet shall that dance be trod!
I will not lift mine arm to war with God
For thee nor all thy words.   Madness most fell
Is on thee, madness wrought by some dread spell,
But not by spell nor leechcraft to be cured!

CHORUS

Grey prophet, worthy of Phoebus is thy word,
And wise in honouring Bromios, our great God

CADMUS

My son, right well Teiresias points thy road.
Oh, make thine habitation here with us,
Not lonely, against men's uses.   Hazardous
Is this quick bird-like beating of thy thought
Where no thought dwells.—Grant that this God be naught,
Yet let that Naught be Somewhat in thy mouth;
Lie boldly, and say He Is!   So north and south
Shall marvel, how there sprang a thing divine
From Semelê's flesh, and honour all our line.
[*Drawing nearer to* PENTHEUS.

   Is there not blood before thine eyes even now?
Our lost Actaeon's blood, whom long ago
His own red hounds through yonder forest dim
Tore unto death, because he vaunted him
Against most holy Artemis?   Oh, beware,
And let me wreathe thy temples.   Make thy prayer
With us, and bear thee humbly in God's sight.
[*He makes as if to set the wreath on* PENTHEUS' *head.*

PENTHEUS

Down with that hand!   Aroint thee to thy rite,
Nor smear on me thy foul contagion!
[*Turning upon* TEIRESIAS.

                                        This
Thy folly's head and prompter shall not miss
The justice that he needs!—Go, half my guard,
Forth to the rock-seat where he dwells in ward
O'er birds and wonders; rend the stone with crow
And trident; make one wreck of high and low,

And toss his bands to all the winds of air!

    Ha, have I found the way to sting thee, there?
The rest, forth through the town!   And seek amain
This girl-faced stranger, that hath wrought such bane
To all Thebes, preying on our maids and wives.
Seek till ye find; and lead him here in gyves,
Till he be judged and stoned, and weep in blood
The day he troubled Pentheus with his God!

[*The guards set forth in two bodies;* PENTHEUS *goes into the
   Castle.*

TEIRESIAS

Hard heart, how little dost thou know what seed
Thou sowest!   Blind before, and now indeed
Most mad!—Come, Cadmus, let us go our way,
And pray for this our persecutor, pray
For this poor city, that the righteous God
Move not in anger.—Take thine ivy rod
And help my steps, as I help thine.   'Twere ill,
If two old men should fall by the roadway.   Still,
Come what come may, our service shall be done
To Bacchios, the All-Father's mystic son.

    O Pentheus, named of sorrow!   Shall he claim
From all thy house fulfilment of his name,
Old Cadmus?—Nay, I speak not from mine art,
But as I see—blind words and a blind heart!

[*The two Old Men go off towards the Mountain.*

CHORUS

Some Maidens

Thou Immaculate on high;
Thou Recording Purity;
Thou that stoopest, Golden Wing,
Earthward, manward, pitying.

Hearest thou this angry King?
Hearest thou the rage and scorn
　'Gainst the Lord of Many Voices,
Him of mortal mother born,
　　Him in whom man's heart rejoices,
Girt with garlands and with glee,
First in Heaven's sovranty?
　　For his kingdom, it is there,
　　In the dancing and the prayer,
In the music and the laughter,
　　In the vanishing of care,
And of all before and after;
In the Gods' high banquet, when
　　Gleams the grape-blood, flashed to heaven;
Yea, and in the feasts of men
Comes his crownèd slumber; then
　　Pain is dead and hate forgiven!

Others

⌈Loose thy lips from out the rein;⌉
⌊Lift thy wisdom to disdain;⌋
Whatso law thou canst not see,
Scorning; so the end shall be
Uttermost calamity!
'Tis the life of quiet breath,
　'Tis the simple and the true,
Storm nor earthquake shattereth,
　Nor shall aught the house undo
Where they dwell.　For, far away,
Hidden from the eyes of day,
　Watchers are there in the skies,
　That can see man's life, and prize
Deeds well done by things of clay.
　But the world's Wise are not wise,

Claiming more than mortal may.
Life is such a little thing;
    Lo, their present is departed,
And the dreams to which they cling
Come not.   Mad imagining
    Theirs, I ween, and empty-hearted!

Divers Maidens
Where is the Home for me?
O Cyprus, set in the sea,
Aphrodite's home In the soft sea-foam,
    Would I could wend to thee;
Where the wings of the Loves are furled,
And faint the heart of the world.

Aye, unto Paphos' isle,
Where the rainless meadows smile
With riches rolled From the hundred-fold
    Mouths of the far-off Nile,
Streaming beneath the waves
To the roots of the seaward caves.

But a better land is there
Where Olympus cleaves the air,
The high still dell Where the Muses dwell,
    Fairest of all things fair!
Desire is there, and the Crowning of Desire,
And peace to adore thee, thou Spirit of Guiding Fire!

———————————

A God of Heaven is he,
And born in majesty;
Yet hath he mirth In the joy of the Earth,
    And he loveth constantly
Her who brings increase,
The Feeder of Children, Peace.

24

No grudge hath he of the great;
No scorn of the mean estate;
But to all that liveth His wine he giveth,
Griefless, immaculate;
Only on them that spurn
Joy, may his anger burn.

Love thou the Day and the Night;
Be glad of the Dark and the Light;
And avert thine eyes From the lore of the wise,
That have honour in proud men's sight.
The simple nameless herd of Humanity
Hath deeds and faith that are truth enough for me!

[*As the Chorus ceases, a party of the guards return, leading in the midst of them* DIONYSUS, *bound. The* SOLDIER *in command stands forth, as* PENTHEUS, *hearing the tramp of feet, comes out from the Castle.*

SOLDIER

Our quest is finished, and thy prey, O King,
Caught; for the chase was swift, and this wild thing
Most tame; yet never flinched, nor thought to flee,
But held both hands out unresistingly—
No change, no blanching of the wine-red cheek.
He waited while we came, and bade us wreak
All thy decree; yea, laughed, and made my hest
Easy, till I for very shame confessed
And said: 'O stranger, not of mine own will
I bind thee, but his bidding to fulfil
Who sent me.'
                    And those prisoned Maids withal
Whom thou didst seize and bind within the wall
Of thy great dungeon, they are fled, O King,
Free in the woods, a-dance and glorying

To Bromios.   Of their own impulse fell
To earth, men say, fetter and manacle,
And bars slid back untouched of mortal hand.
Yea, full of many wonders to thy land
Is this man come. . . . Howbeit, it lies with thee!

PENTHEUS

Ye are mad!—Unhand him.   Howso swift he be,
My toils are round him and he shall not fly.
[*The guards loose the arms of* DIONYSUS; PENTHEUS *studies
him for a while in silence, then speaks jeeringly.*   DIONYSUS
remains gentle and unafraid.
Marry, a fair shape for a woman's eye,
Sir stranger!   And thou seek'st no more, I ween!
Long curls, withal!   That shows thou ne'er hast been
A wrestler!—down both cheeks so softly tossed
And winsome!   And a white skin!   It hath cost
Thee pains, to please thy damsels with this white
And red of cheeks that never face the light!
[DIONYSUS *is silent.*
Speak, sirrah; tell me first thy name and race.

DIONYSUS

No glory is therein, nor yet disgrace.
Thou hast heard of Tmolus, the bright hill of flowers?

PENTHEUS

Surely; the ridge that winds by Sardis' towers.

DIONYSUS

Thence am I; Lydia was my fatherland.

PENTHEUS

And whence these revelations, that thy band
Spreadeth in Hellas?

DIONYSUS
Their intent and use
Dionysus oped to me, the Child of Zeus.

PENTHEUS (*brutally*)
Is there a Zeus there, that can still beget
Young Gods?

DIONYSUS
Nay, only He whose seal was set
Here in thy Thebes on Semelê.

PENTHEUS
What way
Descended he upon thee?   In full day
Or vision of night?

DIONYSUS
Most clear he stood, and scanned
My soul, and gave his emblems to mine hand.

PENTHEUS
What like be they, these emblems?

DIONYSUS
That may none
Reveal, nor know, save his Elect alone.

PENTHEUS
And what good bring they to the worshipper?

DIONYSUS
Good beyond price, but not for thee to hear.

PENTHEUS

Thou trickster! Thou wouldst prick me on the more
To seek them out!

DIONYSUS

His mysteries abhor
The touch of sin-lovers.

PENTHEUS

And so thine eyes
Saw this God plain; what guise had he?

DIONYSUS

What guise
It liked him. 'Twas not I ordained his shape.

PENTHEUS

Aye, deftly turned again. An idle jape,
And nothing answered!

DIONYSUS

Wise words being brought
To blinded eyes will seem as things of nought.

PENTHEUS

And comest thou first to Thebes, to have thy God
Established?

DIONYSUS

Nay; all Barbary hath trod
His dance ere this.

PENTHEUS

A low blind folk, I ween,
Beside our Hellenes!

DIONYSUS
              Higher and more keen
In this thing, though their ways are not thy way.

PENTHEUS
How is thy worship held, by night or day?

DIONYSUS
Most oft by night; 'tis a majestic thing.
The darkness.

PENTHEUS
              Ha! with women worshipping?
'Tis craft and rottenness!

DIONYSUS
                    By day no less,
Whoso will seek may find unholiness.

PENTHEUS
Enough!   Thy doom is fixed, for false pretence
Corrupting Thebes.

DIONYSUS
              Not mine; but thine, for dense
Blindness of heart, and for blaspheming God!

PENTHEUS
A ready knave it is, and brazen-browed,
This mystery-priest!

DIONYSUS
              Come, say what it shall be,
My doom; what dire thing wilt thou do to me?

PENTHEUS

First, shear that delicate curl that dangles there.
[*He beckons to the soldiers, who approach* DIONYSUS.

DIONYSUS

I have vowed it to my God; 'tis holy air.
[*The soldiers cut off the tress.*

PENTHEUS

Next, yield me up thy staff!

DIONYSUS

Raise thine own hand
To take it.   This is Dionysus' wand.
[PENTHEUS *takes the staff*

PENTHEUS

Last, I will hold thee prisoned here.

DIONYSUS

My Lord
God will unloose me, when I speak the word.

PENTHEUS

He may, if e'er again amid his bands
Of saints he hears thy voice!

DIONYSUS

Even now he stands
Close here, and sees all that I suffer.

PENTHEUS

What!
Where is he? For mine eyes discern him not.

DIONYSUS

Where I am! 'Tis thine own impurity
That veils him from thee.

PENTHEUS

                    The dog jeers at me!
At me and Thebes!   Bind him!
[*The soldiers begin to bind him.*

DIONYSUS

                        I charge ye, bind
Me not!   I having vision and ye blind!

PENTHEUS

And I, with better right, say bind the more!
[*The soldiers obey.*

DIONYSUS

Thou knowest not what life thou livest, nor
What deed thou doest, nor what man thou art!

PENTHEUS (*mocking*)

Agâvê's son, and on the father's part
Echîon's, hight Pentheus!

DIONYSUS

                    So let it be,
A name fore-written to calamity!

PENTHEUS

Away, and tie him where the steeds are tied;
Aye, let him lie in the manger!—There abide
And stare into the darkness!—And this rout
Of womankind that clusters thee about,

31

Thy ministers of worship, are my slaves!
It may be I will sell them o'er the waves,
Hither and thither; else they shall be set
To labour at my distaffs, and forget
Their timbrel and their songs of dawning day!

DIONYSUS

I go; for that which may not be, I may
Not suffer!   Yet for this thy sin, lo, He
Whom thou deniest cometh after thee
For recompense.   Yea, in thy wrong to us,
Thou hast cast Him into thy prison-house!

[DIONYSUS, *without his wand, his hair shorn, and his arms
   tightly bound, is led off by the guards to his dungeon.* PEN-
   THEUS *returns into the Palace.*

CHORUS

Some Maidens

Acheloüs' roaming daughter,
Holy Dircê, virgin water,
Bathed he not of old in thee,
The Babe of God, the Mystery?
When from out the fire immortal
   To himself his God did take him,
   To his own flesh, and bespake him:
" Enter now life's second portal,
Motherless Mystery; lo, I break
Mine own body for thy sake,
   Thou of the Twofold Door, and seal thee
Mine, O Bromios,"—thus he spake—
   " And to this thy land reveal thee."

All

Still my prayer toward thee quivers,
　　Dircê, still to thee I hie me;
Why, O Blessèd among Rivers,
　　Wilt thou fly me and deny me?
　　　　By His own joy I vow,
　　　　By the grape upon the bough,
Thou shalt seek Him in the midnight, thou shalt love Him,
　　even now!

Other Maidens

Dark and of the dark impassioned
Is this Pentheus' blood; yea, fashioned
Of the Dragon, and his birth
From Echîon, child of Earth.
He is no man, but a wonder;
　　Did the Earth-Child not beget him,
　　As a red Giant, to set him
Against God, against the Thunder?
He will bind me for his prize,
Me, the Bride of Dionyse;
　　And my priest, my friend, is taken
Even now, and buried lies;
　　In the dark he lies forsaken!

All

Lo, we race with death, we perish,
　　Dionysus, here before thee!
Dost thou mark us not, nor cherish,
　　Who implore thee, and adore thee?
　　　　Hither down Olympus' side,
　　　　Come, O Holy One defied,
Be thy golden wand uplifted o'er the tyrant in his pride!

A Maiden

Oh, where art thou?   In thine own
Nysa, thou our help alone?
O'er fierce beasts in orient lands
        Doth thy thronging thyrsus wave,
        By the high Corycian Cave,
Or where stern Olympus stands;
In the elm-woods and the oaken,
        There where Orpheus harped of old,
    And the trees awoke and knew him,
    And the wild things gathered to him,
As he sang amid the broken
        Glens his music manifold?
Blessed Land of Piërie,
Dionysus loveth thee;
    He will come to thee ·vith dancing,
Come with joy and mystery;
With the Maenads at his hest
Winding, winding to the West;
    Cross the flood of swiftly glancing
Axios in majesty;
Cross the Lydias, the giver
    Of good gifts and waving green;
Cross that Father-Stream of story,
Through a land of steeds and glory
Rolling, bravest, fairest River
        E'er of mortals seen!

A VOICE WITHIN
Io!   Io!
Awake, ye damsels; hear my cry,
        Calling my Chosen; hearken ye

A MAIDEN
Who speaketh?   Oh, what echoes thus?

34

ANOTHER

A Voice, a Voice, that calleth us!

THE VOICE

Be of good cheer!   Lo, it is I,
    The Child of Zeus and Semelê.

A MAIDEN

O Master, Master, it is Thou!

ANOTHER

O Holy Voice, be with us now!

THE VOICE

Spirit of the Chained Earthquake,
Hear my word; awake, awake!

[*An Earthquake suddenly shakes the pillars of the Castle.*

A MAIDEN

Ha! what is coming?   Shall the hall
Of Pentheus racked in ruin fall?

LEADER

Our God is in the house!   Ye maids adore Him!

CHORUS

                    We adore Him all!

THE VOICE

Unveil the Lightning's eye; arouse
The fire that sleeps, against this house!

[*Fire leaps up on the Tomb of Semelê.*

35

A MAIDEN

Ah, saw ye, marked ye there the flame
From Semelê's enhallowed sod
Awakened? Yea, the Death that came
Ablaze from heaven of old, the same
Hot splendour of the shaft of God?

LEADER

Oh, cast ye, cast ye, to the earth! The Lord
Cometh against this house! Oh, cast ye down,
Ye trembling damsels; He, our own adored,
God's Child hath come, and all is overthrown!

[*The Maidens cast themselves upon the ground, their eyes earthward.* DIONYSUS, *alone and unbound, enters from the Castle.*

DIONYSUS

Ye Damsels of the Morning Hills, why lie ye thus dismayed?
Ye marked him, then, our Master, and the mighty hand he laid
On tower and rock, shaking the house of Pentheus?—But arise,
And cast the trembling from your flesh, and lift untroubled eyes.

LEADER

O Light in Darkness, is it thou? O Priest is this thy face?
My heart leaps out to greet thee from the deep of loneliness.

DIONYSUS

Fell ye so quick despairing, when beneath the Gate I passed?
Should the gates of Pentheus quell me, or his darkness make me fast?

36

LEADER

Oh, what was left if thou wert gone? What could I but despair?

How hast thou 'scaped the man of sin? Who freed thee from the snare?

DIONYSUS

I had no pain nor peril; 'twas mine own hand set me free.

LEADER

Thine arms were gyvèd!

DIONYSUS

Nay, no gyve, no touch, was laid on me!

'Twas there I mocked him, in his gyves, and gave him dreams for food.

For when he led me down, behold, before the stall there stood

A Bull of Offering. And this King, he bit his lips, and straight

Fell on and bound it, hoof and limb, with gasping wrath and sweat.

And I sat watching!—Then a Voice; and lo, our Lord was come,

And the house shook, and a great flame stood o'er his mother's tomb.

And Pentheus hied this way and that, and called his thralls amain

For water, lest his roof-tree burn; and all toiled, all in vain.

Then deemed a-sudden I was gone; and left his fire, and sped

Back to the prison portals, and his lifted sword shone red.

But there, methinks, the God had wrought—I speak but as I guess—

Some dream-shape in mine image; for he smote at emptiness,

37

Stabbed in the air, and strove in wrath, as though 'twere me
    he slew.

Then 'mid his dreams God smote him yet again! He
    overthrew

All that high house. And there in wreck for evermore
    it lies,

That the day of this my bondage may be sore in Pentheus'
    eyes!

  And now his sword is fallen, and he lies outworn and wan

Who dared to rise against his God in wrath, being but
    man.

And I uprose and left him, and in all peace took my path

Forth to my Chosen, recking light of Pentheus and his
    wrath.

  But soft, methinks a footstep sounds even now within
    the hall;

'Tis he; how think ye he will stand, and what words speak
    withal?

I will endure him gently, though he come in fury hot.

For still are the ways of Wisdom, and her temper trembleth
    not!

[*Enter* PENTHEUS *in fury.*

PENTHEUS

It is too much! This Eastern knave hath slipped
His prison, whom I held but now, hard gripped
In bondage.—Ha! 'Tis he!—What, sirrah, how
Show'st thou before my portals?
[*He advances furiously upon him.*

DIONYSUS

              Softly thou!
And set a quiet carriage to thy rage

PENTHEUS

How comest thou here?   How didst thou break thy cage?
Speak!

DIONYSUS

　　　Said I not, or didst thou mark not me,
There was One living that should set me free?

PENTHEUS

Who?   Ever wilder are these tales of thine.

DIONYSUS

He who first made for man the clustered vine.

PENTHEUS

I scorn him and his vines!

DIONYSUS

　　　　　For Dionyse
'Tis well; for in thy scorn his glory lies.

PENTHEUS (to his guard)

Go swift to all the towers, and bar withal
Each gate!

DIONYSUS

　　　What, cannot God o'erleap a wall?

PENTHEUS

Oh, wit thou hast, save where thou needest it!

DIONYSUS

Whereso it most imports, there is my wit!—
Nay, peace!   Abide till he who hasteth from

The mountain side with news for thee, be come.
We will not fly, but wait on thy command.
[*Enter suddenly and in haste a Messenger from the Mountain.*

MESSENGER

Great Pentheus, Lord of all this Theban land,
I come from high Kithaeron, where the frore
Snow spangles gleam and cease not evermore. . . .

PENTHEUS

And what of import may thy coming bring?

MESSENGER

I have seen the Wild White Women there, O King,
Whose fleet limbs darted arrow-like but now
From Thebes away, and come to tell thee how
They work strange deeds and passing marvel.   Yet
I first would learn thy pleasure.   Shall I set
My whole tale forth, or veil the stranger part?
Yea, Lord, I fear the swiftness of thy heart,
Thine edgèd wrath and more than royal soul.

PENTHEUS

Thy tale shall nothing scathe thee.—Tell the whole.
It skills not to be wroth with honesty.
Nay, if thy news of them be dark, 'tis he
Shall pay it, who bewitched and led them on.

MESSENGER

Our herded kine were moving in the dawn
Up to the peaks, the greyest, coldest time,
When the first rays steal earthward, and the rime
Yields, when I saw three bands of them.   The one
Autonoë led, one Ino, one thine own

Mother, Agâvê.   There beneath the trees
Sleeping they lay, like wild things flung at ease
In the forest; one half sinking on a bed
Of deep pine greenery; one with careless head
Amid the fallen oak leaves; all most cold
In purity—not as thy tale was told
Of wine-cups and wild music and the chase
For love amid the forest's loneliness.
Then rose the Queen Agâvê suddenly
Amid her band, and gave the God's wild cry,
"Awake, ye Bacchanals! I hear the sound
Of hornèd kine.   Awake ye! "—Then, all round,
Alert, the warm sleep fallen from their eyes,
A marvel of swift ranks I saw them rise,
Dames young and old, and gentle maids unwed
Among them.   O'er their shoulders first they shed
Their tresses, and caught up the fallen fold
Of mantles where some clasp had loosened hold,
And girt the dappled fawn-skins in with long
Quick snakes that hissed and writhed with quivering tongue.
And one a young fawn held, and one a wild
Wolf cub, and fed them with white milk, and smiled
In love, young mothers with a mother's breast
And babes at home forgotten!   Then they pressed
Wreathed ivy round their brows, and oaken sprays
And flowering bryony.   And one would raise
Her wand and smite the rock, and straight a jet
Of quick bright water came.   Another set
Her thyrsus in the bosomed earth, and there
Was red wine that the God sent up to her,
A darkling fountain.   And if any lips
Sought whiter draughts, with dipping finger-tips
They pressed the sod, and gushing from the ground
Came springs of milk.   And reed-wands ivy-crowned

Ran with sweet honey, drop by drop.—O King,
Hadst thou been there, as I, and seen this thing,
With prayer and most high wonder hadst thou gone
To adore this God whom now thou rail'st upon!

   Howbeit, the kine-wardens and shepherds straight
Came to one place, amazed, and held debate;
And one being there who walked the streets and scanned
The ways of speech, took lead of them whose hand
Knew but the slow soil and the solemn hill,
And flattering spoke, and asked: " Is it your will,
Masters, we stay the mother of the King.
Agâvê, from her lawless worshipping,
And win us royal thanks? "—And this seemed good
To all; and through the branching underwood
We hid us, cowering in the leaves.   And there
Through the appointed hour they made their prayer
And worship of the Wand, with one accord
Of heart and cry—" Iacchos, Bromios, Lord,
God of God born! "—And all the mountain felt,
And worshipped with them; and the wild things knelt
And ramped and gloried, and the wilderness
Was filled with moving voices and dim stress.

   Soon, as it chanced, beside my thicket-close
The Queen herself passed dancing, and I rose
And sprang to seize her.   But she turned her face
Upon me: " Ho, my rovers of the chase,
My wild White Hounds, we are hunted!   Up, each rod
And follow, follow, for our Lord and God! "
Thereat, for fear they tear us, all we fled
Amazed; and on, with hand unweaponèd
They swept toward our herds that browsed the green
Hill grass.   Great uddered kine then hadst thou seen
Bellowing in sword-like hands that cleave and tear,
A live steer riven asunder, and the air

42

Tossed with rent ribs or limbs of cloven tread.
And flesh upon the branches, and a red
Rain from the deep green pines.   Yea, bulls of pride,
Horns swift to rage, were fronted and aside
Flung stumbling, by those multitudinous hands
Dragged pitilessly.   And swifter were the bands
Of garbèd flesh and bone unbound withal
Than on thy royal eyes the lids may fall.

Then on like birds, by their own speed upborne,
They swept toward the plains of waving corn
That lie beside Asôpus' banks, and bring
To Thebes the rich fruit of her harvesting.
On Hysiae and Erythrae that lie nursed
Amid Kithaeron's bowering rocks, they burst
Destroying, as a foeman's army comes.
They caught up little children from their homes,
High on their shoulders, babes unheld, that swayed
And laughed and fell not; all a wreck they made;
Yea, bronze and iron did shatter, and in play
Struck hither and thither, yet no wound had they;
Caught fire from out the hearths, yea, carried hot
Flames in their tresses and were scorchèd not!

The village folk in wrath took spear and sword,
And turned upon the Bacchae.   Then, dread Lord,
The wonder was.   For spear not barbèd brand
Could scathe nor touch the damsels; but the Wand,
The soft and wreathèd wand their white hands sped,
Blasted those men and quelled them, and they fled
Dizzily.   Sure some God was in these things!

And the holy women back to those strange springs
Returned, that God had sent them when the day
Dawned, on the upper heights; and washed away
The stain of battle.   And those girdling snakes
Hissed out to lap the waterdrops from cheeks

And hair and breast.

            Therefore I counsel thee,
O King, receive this Spirit, whoe'er he be,
To Thebes in glory.   Greatness manifold
Is all about him; and the tale is told
That this is he who first to man did give
The grief-assuaging vine.   Oh, let him live;
For if he die, then Love herself is slain,
And nothing joyous in the world again!

LEADER

Albeit I tremble, and scarce may speak my thought
To a king's face, yet will I hide it not.
Dionyse is God, no God more true nor higher!

PENTHEUS

It bursts hard by us, like a smothered fire,
This frenzy of Bacchic women!   All my land
Is made their mock.—This needs an iron hand!
  Ho, Captain!   Quick to the Electran Gate;
Bid gather all my men-at-arms thereat;
Call all that spur the charger, all who know
To wield the orbèd targe or bend the bow;
We march to war!—'Fore God, shall women dare
Such deeds against us?   'Tis too much to bear!

DIONYSUS

Thou mark'st me not, O King, and holdest light
My solemn words; yet, in thine own despite,
I warn thee still.   Lift thou not up thy spear
Against a God, but hold thy peace, and fear
His wrath!   He will not brook it, if thou fright
His Chosen from the hills of their delight.

44

PENTHEUS

Peace, thou! And if for once thou hast slipped thy chain,
Give thanks!—Or shall I knot thine arms again?

DIONYSUS

Better to yield him prayer and sacrifice
Than kick against the pricks, since Dionyse
Is God, and thou but mortal.

PENTHEUS

That will I!
Yea, sacrifice of women's blood, to cry
His name through all Kithaeron!

DIONYSUS

Ye shall fly,
All, and abase your shields of bronzen rim
Before their wands.

PENTHEUS

There is no way with him,
This stranger that so dogs us! Well or ill
I may entreat him, he must babble still!

DIONYSUS

Wait, good my friend! These crooked matters may
Even yet be straightened.
[PENTHEUS *has started as though to seek his army at the gate.*

PENTHEUS

Aye, if I obey
Mine own slaves' will; how else?

DIONYSUS

Myself will lead
The damsels hither, without sword or steed.

PENTHEUS

How now?—This is some plot against me!

DIONYSUS
                                                              What
Dost fear?   Only to save thee do I plot.

PENTHEUS

It is some compact ye have made, whereby
To dance these hills for ever!

DIONYSUS
                        Verily,
That is my compact, plighted with my Lord!

PENTHEUS (*turning from him*)

Ho, armourers!   Bring forth my shield and sword!—
And thou, be silent!

DIONYSUS
(*after regarding him fixedly, speaks with resignation*)
                        Ah!—Have then thy will!
[*He fixes his eyes upon* PENTHEUS *again, while the armourers
    bring out his armour; then speaks in a tone of command.*
Man, thou wouldst fain behold them on the hill
Praying!

PENTHEUS
(*who during the rest of this scene, with a few exceptions, simply
    speaks the thoughts that* DIONYSUS *puts into him, losing
    power over his own mind*)
                        That would I, though it cost me all
The gold of Thebes!

46

DIONYSUS

So much?　Thou art quick to fall
To such great longing.

PENTHEUS
(*somewhat bewildered at what he has said*)

Aye; 'twould grieve me much
To see them flown with wine.

DIONYSUS

Yet cravest thou such
A sight as would much grieve thee?

PENTHEUS

Yes; I fain
Would watch, ambushed among the pines.

DIONYSUS

'Twere vain
To hide.　They soon will track thee out.

PENTHEUS

Well said!
'Twere best done openly.

DIONYSUS

Wilt thou be led
By me, and try the venture?

PENTHEUS

Aye, indeed!
Lead on.　Why should we tarry?

DIONYSUS
                              First we need
A rich and trailing robe of fine-linen
To gird thee.

PENTHEUS
                    Nay; am I a woman, then,
And man no more?

DIONYSUS
                         Wouldst have them slay thee dead?
No man may see their mysteries.

PENTHEUS
                                   Well said!—
I marked thy subtle temper long ere now.

DIONYSUS
'Tis Dionyse that prompteth me.

PENTHEUS
                                        And how
Mean'st thou the further plan?

DIONYSUS
                                   First take thy way
Within.   I will array thee.

PENTHEUS
                         What array?
The woman's?   Nay, I will not.

DIONYSUS
                                   Doth it change
So soon, all thy desire to see this strange
Adoring?

48

PENTHEUS

Wait!   What garb wilt thou bestow
About me?

DIONYSUS

First a long tress dangling low
Beneath thy shoulders.

PENTHEUS
Aye, and next?

DIONYSUS

The said
Robe, falling to thy feet; and on thine head
A snood.

PENTHEUS
And after?   Hast thou aught beyond?

DIONYSUS
Surely; the dappled fawn-skin and the wand.

PENTHEUS (*after a struggle with himself*)
Enough!   I cannot wear a robe and snood.

DIONYSUS
Wouldst liefer draw the sword and spill men's blood?

PENTHEUS (*again doubting*)
True, that were evil.—Aye; 'tis best to go
First to some place of watch.

DIONYSUS

Far wiser so,
Than seek by wrath wrath's bitter recompense.

D   49

PENTHEUS

What of the city streets?   Canst lead me hence
Unseen of any?

DIONYSUS
Lonely and untried
Thy path from hence shall be, and I thy guide!

PENTHEUS

I care for nothing, so these Bacchanals
Triumph not against me! . . .Forward to my halls
Within!—I will ordain what seemeth best.

DIONYSUS

So be it, O King!   'Tis mine to obey thine hest,
Whate'er it be.

PENTHEUS
(after hesitating once more and waiting)
Well, I will go—perchance
To march and scatter them with serried lance,
Perchance to take thy plan. . . . I know not yet.
[*Exit* PENTHEUS *into the Castle.*

DIONYSUS

Damsels, the lion walketh to the net.
He finds his Bacchae now, and sees and dies,
And pays for all his sin!—O Dionyse,
This is thine hour and thou not far away.
Grant us our vengeance!—First, O Master, stay
The course of reason in him, and instil
A foam of madness.   Let his seeing will,
Which ne'er had stooped to put thy vesture on,
Be darkened, till the deed is lightly done.
Grant likewise that he find through all his streets
Loud scorn, this man of wrath and bitter threats

That made Thebes tremble, led in woman's guise.
   I go to fold that robe of sacrifice
On Pentheus, that shall deck him to the dark,
His mother's gift!—So shall he learn and mark
God's true Son, Dionyse, in fulness God,
Most fearful, yet to man most soft of mood.
[*Exit* DIONYSUS, *following* PENTHEUS *into the Castle.*

CHORUS
Some Maidens

Will they ever come to me, ever again,
      The long long dances,
On through the dark till the dawn-stars wane?
Shall I feel the dew on my throat, and the stream
Of wind in my hair?   Shall our white feet gleam
      In the dim expanses?
Oh, feet of a fawn to the greenwood fled,
   Alone in the grass and the loveliness;
Leap of the hunted, no more in dread,
   Beyond the snares and the deadly press:
Yet a voice still in the distance sounds,
A shout, a threat, and a haste of hounds;
O wildly labouring, fiercely fleet,
   Onward yet by river and glen . . .
Is it joy or terror, ye storm-swift feet?
   To the dear lone lands untroubled of men,
Where no voice sounds, and amid the shadowy green
The little things of the woodland live unseen.

What else is Wisdom?   What of man's endeavour
   Or God's high grace, so lovely and so great?
   To stand from fear set free, to breathe and wait;
   To hold a hand uplifted over Hate;
And shall not loveliness be loved for ever?

51

Others

O Strength of God, slow art thou and still,
          Yet failest never!
On them that worship the Ruthless Will,
On them that dream, doth His judgment wait,
Dreams of the proud man, making great
          And greater ever,
Things which are not of God.   In wide
     And devious coverts, hunter-wise,
He coucheth Time's unhasting stride,
     Following, following, him whose eyes
Look not to Heaven.   For all is vain,
The pulse of the heart, the plot of the brain,
That striveth beyond the laws that live.
And is thy Faith so much to give,
Is it so hard a thing to see,
That the Spirit of God, whate'er it be,
The Law that abides and changes not, ages long,
The Eternal and Nature-born—these things be strong?

What else is Wisdom?   What of man's endeavour
     Or God's high grace so lovely and so great?
     To stand from fear set free, to breathe and wait;
     To hold a hand uplifted over Hate;
And shall not Loveliness be loved for ever?

LEADER

Happy he, on the weary sea,
Who hath fled the tempest and won the haven.
     Happy whoso hath risen, free,
Above his striving.   For strangely graven
     Is the orb of life, that one and another
     In gold and power may outpass his brother.
     And men in their millions float and flow

And seethe with a million hopes as leaven;
>   And they win their will, or they miss their will,
>   And the hopes are dead or are pined for still;
>   But whoe'er can know,
>   As the long days go,
That To Live is happy, hath found his Heaven!

[*Re-enter* DIONYSUS *from the Castle.*

DIONYSUS

O eye that cravest sights thou must not see,
O heart athirst for that which slakes not! Thee,
Pentheus, I call; forth and be seen, in guise
Of woman, Maenad, saint of Dionyse,
To spy upon His Chosen and thine own
Mother!
[*Enter* PENTHEUS, *clad like a Bacchanal, and strangely excited,*
a spirit of Bacchic madness overshadowing him.
>   Thy shape, methinks, is like to one
Of Cadmus' royal maids!

PENTHEUS

>   Yea; and mine eye
Is bright! Yon sun shines twofold in the sky,
Thebes twofold and the Wall of Seven Gates. . . .
And is it a Wild Bull this, that walks and waits
Before me? There are horns upon thy brow!
What art thou, man or beast? For surely now
The Bull is on thee!

DIONYSUS

>   He who erst was wrath,
Goes with us now in gentleness. He hath
Unsealed thine eyes to see what thou shouldst see.

PENTHEUS

Say; stand I not as Ino stands, or she
Who bore me?

DIONYSUS

When I look on thee, it seems
I see their very selves.—But stay; why streams
That lock abroad, not where I laid it, crossed
Under the coif?

PENTHEUS

I did it, as I tossed
My head in dancing, to and fro, and cried
His holy music!

DIONYSUS (*tending him*)

It shall soon be tied
Aright. 'Tis mine to tend thee. . . . Nay, but stand
With head straight.

PENTHEUS

In the hollow of thy hand
I lay me. Deck me as thou wilt.

DIONYSUS

Thy zone
Is loosened likewise; and the folded gown
Not evenly falling to the feet.

PENTHEUS

'Tis so,
By the right foot. But here, methinks, they flow
In one straight line to the heel.

DIONYSUS (*while tending him*)

And if thou prove
Their madness true, aye, more than true, what love
And thanks hast thou for me?

54

PENTHEUS (*not listening to him*)
                              In my right hand
Is it, or thus, that I should bear the wand,
To be most like to them?

DIONYSUS
                              Up let it swing
In the right hand, timed with the right foot's spring. . . .
'Tis well thy heart is changed.

PENTHEUS (*more wildly*)
                              What strength is this!
Kithaeron's steeps and all that in them is—
How say'st thou?—Could my shoulders lift the whole.

DIONYSUS
Surely they can, if so thou wilt! Thy soul,
Being once so sick, now stands as it should stand.

PENTHEUS
Shall it be bars of iron? Or this bare hand
And shoulder to the crags, to wrench them down?

DIONYSUS
Wouldst wreck the Nymphs' wild temples, and the brown
Rocks where Pan pipes at noonday?

PENTHEUS
                              Nay; not I!
Force is not well with women. I will lie
Hid in the pine-brake.
                    DIONYSUS
                    Even as fits a spy
On holy and fearful things, so shalt thou lie!

PENTHEUS (*with a laugh*)

They lie there now, methinks—the wild birds, caught
By love among the leaves, and fluttering not!

DIONYSUS

It may be.   That is what thou goest to see,
Aye, and to trap them—so they trap not thee!

PENTHEUS

Forth through the Thebans' town!   I am their king,
Aye, their one Man, seeing I dare this thing!

DIONYSUS

Yea, thou shalt bear their burden, thou alone;
Therefore thy trial awaiteth thee.—But on;
With me into thine ambush shalt thou come
Unscathed; then let another bear thee home!

PENTHEUS

The Queen, my mother.

DIONYSUS

Marked of every eye.

PENTHEUS

For that I go!

DIONYSUS

Thou shalt be borne on high.

PENTHEUS

That were like pride

DIONYSUS

Thy mother's hands shall share

Thy carrying.

PENTHEUS

Nay; I need not such soft care.

DIONYSUS

So soft?

PENTHEUS

Whate'er it be, I have earned it well.
[*Exit* PENTHEUS *towards the Mountain.*

DIONYSUS

Fell, fell art thou; and to a doom so fell
Thou walkest, that thy name from South to North
Shall shine, a sign for ever.—Reach thou forth
Thine arms, Agâvê, now, and ye dark-browed
Cadmeian sisters!   Greet this prince so proud
To the high ordeal, where save God and me,
None walks unscathed!—The rest this day shall see.
[*Exit* DIONYSUS *following* PENTHEUS.

CHORUS
Some Maidens

O hounds raging and blind,
    Up by the mountain road,
Sprites of the maddened mind,
    To the wild Maids of God;
Fill with your rage their eyes,
    Rage at the rage unblest,
Watching in woman's guise,
    The spy upon God's Possessed.

A Bacchanal

Who shall be first, to mark
    Eyes in the rock that spy,
Eyes in the pine-tree dark—
    Is it his mother?—and cry:

"Lo, what is this that comes,
　　Haunting, troubling still,
Even in our heights, our homes,
　　The wild Maids of the Hill?
What flesh bare this child?
　　Never on woman's breast
Changeling so evil smiled;
　　Man is he not, but Beast!
Lion-shape of the wild,
　　Gorgon-breed of the waste!"

All the Chorus

Hither, for doom and deed!
　　Hither with lifted sword,
　　Justice, Wrath of the Lord,
Come in our visible need!
Smite till the throat shall bleed,
Smite till the heart shall bleed,
Him the tyrannous, lawless, Godless, Echîon's earthborn seed!

Other Maidens

Tyrannously hath he trod;
　　Marched him, in Law's despite,
Against thy Light, O God,
　　Yea, and thy Mother's Light;
Girded him, falsely bold,
　　Blinded in craft, to quell
And by man's violence hold
　　Things unconquerable.

A Bacchanal

A strait pitiless mind
　　Is death unto godliness;
And to feel in human kind
　　Life, and a pain the less.

Knowledge, we are not foes!
I seek thee diligently;
But the world with a great wind blows,
    Shining, and not from thee;
Blowing to beautiful things,
    On, amid dark and light,
Till Life, through the trammellings
    Of Laws that are not the Right,
Breaks, clean and pure, and sings
    Glorying to God in the height!

All the Chorus
Hither for doom and deed!
    Hither with lifted sword,
    Justice, Wrath of the Lord,
Come in our visible need!
Smite till the throat shall bleed,
Smite till the heart shall bleed,
Him the tyrannous, lawless, Godless, Echîon's earthborn
    seed!

LEADER
Appear, appear, whatso thy shape or name,
    O Mountain Bull, Snake of the Hundred Heads,
        Lion of Burning Flame!
O God, Beast, Mystery, come!   Thy mystic maids
Are hunted!—Blast their hunter with thy breath,
        Cast o'er his head thy snare;
And laugh aloud and drag him to his death,
    Who stalks thy herded madness in its lair!

[*Enter hastily a* MESSENGER *from the Mountain, pale and
    distraught.*

MESSENGER
Woe to the house once blest in Hellas!   Woe
To thee, old King Sidonian, who didst sow

The dragon-seed on Ares' bloody lea!
Alas, even thy slaves must weep for thee.

LEADER

News from the mountain?—Speak!   How hath it sped?

MESSENGER

Pentheus, my king, Echîon's son, is dead!

LEADER

All hail, God of the Voice,
Manifest ever more!

MESSENGER

What say'st thou?—And how strange thy tone, as though
In joy at this my master's overthrow!

LEADER

With fierce joy I rejoice,
Child of a savage shore;
For the chains of my prison are broken, and the dread where
I cowered of yore!

MESSENGER

And deem'st thou Thebes so beggared, so forlorn
Of manhood, as to sit beneath thy scorn?

LEADER

Thebes hath o'er me no sway!
None save Him I obey,
Dionysus, Child of the Highest, Him I obey and adore!

MESSENGER

One can forgive thee.—Yet 'tis no fair thing,
Maids, to rejoice in a man's suffering.

LEADER

Speak of the mountain side!
Tell us the doom he died,
The sinner smitten to death, even where his sin was sore!

MESSENGER

We climbed beyond the utmost habitings
Of Theban shepherds, passed Asôpus' springs,
And struck into the land of rock on dim
Kithaeron—Pentheus, and, attending him,
I, and the Stranger who should guide our way.
Then first in a green dell we stopped, and lay,
Lips dumb and feet unmoving, warily
Watching, to be unseen and yet to see.

A narrow glen it was, by crags o'ertowered,
Torn through by tossing waters, and there lowered
A shadow of great pines over it.　And there
The Maenad maidens sate; in toil they were,
Busily glad.　Some with an ivy chain
Tricked a worn wand to toss its locks again;
Some, wild in joyance, like young steeds set free,
Made answering songs of mystic melody.

But my poor master saw not the great band
Before him.　"Stranger," cried he, "where we stand
Mine eyes can reach not these false saints of thine.
Mount we the bank, or some high-shouldered pine,
And I shall see their follies clear!"　At that
There came a marvel.　For the Stranger straight
Touched a great pine-tree's high and heavenward crown,
And lower, lower, lower, urged it down
To the herbless floor.　Round like a bending bow,
Or slow wheel's rim a joiner forces to,
So in those hands that tough and mountain stem
Bowed slow—oh, strength not mortal dwelt in them!—

To the very earth. And there he set the King.
And slowly, lest it cast him in its spring,
Let back the young and straining tree, till high
It towered again amid the towering sky;
And Pentheus in the branches! Well, I ween,
He saw the Maenads then, and well was seen!
For scarce was he aloft, when suddenly
There was no Stranger any more with me,
But out of Heaven a Voice—oh, what voice else?—
'Twas He that called! "Behold, O damosels,
I bring ye him who turneth to despite
Both me and ye, and darkeneth my great Light.
'Tis yours to avenge!" So spake he, and there came
'Twixt earth and sky a pillar of high flame.
And silence took the air, and no leaf stirred
In all the forest dell. Thou hadst not heard
In that vast silence any wild thing's cry.
And up they sprang; but with bewildered eye,
Agaze and listening, scarce yet hearing true.
Then came the Voice again. And when they knew
Their God's clear call, old Cadmus' royal brood,
Up, like wild pigeons startled in a wood,
On flying feet they came, his mother blind,
Agâvê, and her sisters, and behind
All the wild crowd, more deeply maddened then,
Through the angry rocks and torrent-tossing glen,
Until they spied him in the dark pine-tree:
Then climbed a crag hard by and furiously
Some sought to stone him, some their wands would fling
Lance-wise aloft, in cruel targeting.
But none could strike. The height o'ertopped their rage,
And there he clung, unscathed, as in a cage
Caught. And of all their strife no end was found.
Then, "Hither," cried Agâvê; "stand we round

And grip the stem, my Wild Ones, till we take
This climbing cat-o'-the-mount! He shall not make
A tale of God's high dances!" Out then shone
Arm upon arm, past count, and closed upon
The pine, and gripped; and the ground gave, and down
It reeled. And that high sitter from the crown
Of the green pine-top, with a shrieking cry
Fell, as his mind grew clear, and there hard by
Was horror visible. 'Twas his mother stood
O'er him, first priestess of those rites of blood.
He tore the coif, and from his head away
Flung it, that she might know him, and not slay
To her own misery. He touched the wild
Cheek, crying: " Mother, it is I, thy child,
Thy Pentheus, born thee in Echîon's hall!
Have mercy, Mother! Let it not befall
Through sin of mine, that thou shouldst slay thy son!"
    But she, with lips a-foam and eyes that run
Like leaping fire, with thoughts that ne'er should be
On earth, possessed by Bacchios utterly,
Stays not nor hears. Round his left arm she put
Both hands, set hard against his side her foot,
Drew . . . and the shoulder severed!—Not by might
Of arm, but easily, as the God made light
Her hand's essay. And at the other side
Was Ino rending; and the torn flesh cried,
And on Autonoë pressed, and all the crowd
Of ravening arms. Yea, all the air was loud
With groans that faded into sobbing breath,
Dim shrieks, and joy, and triumph-cries of death.
And here was borne a severed arm, and there
A hunter's booted foot; white bones lay bare
With rending; and swift hands ensanguinèd
Tossed as in sport the flesh of Pentheus dead.

His body lies afar.   The precipice
Hath part, and parts in many an interstice
Lurk of the tangled woodland—no light quest
To find.   And, ah, the head!   Of all the rest,
His mother hath it, pierced upon a wand,
As one might pierce a lion's, and through the land,
Leaving her sisters in their dancing place,
Bears it on high.   Yea, to these walls her face
Was set, exulting in her deed of blood,
Calling upon her Bromios, her God,
Her Comrade, Fellow-Render of the Prey,
Her All-Victorious, to whom this day
She bears in triumph . . . her own broken heart!

For me, after that sight, I will depart
Before Agâvê comes.—Oh, to fulfil
God's laws, and have no thought beyond His will,
Is man's best treasure.   Aye, and wisdom true,
Methinks, for things of dust to cleave unto!
[*The* MESSENGER *departs into the Castle.*

CHORUS

Some Maidens
Weave ye the dance, and call
Praise to God!
Bless ye the Tyrant's fall!
Down is trod
Pentheus, the Dragon's Seed!
Wore he the woman's weed?
Clasped he his death indeed,
Clasped the rod?

A Bacchanal
Yea, the wild ivy lapt him, and the doomed
Wild Bull of Sacrifice before him loomed.

64

Others
Ye who did Bromios scorn,
　　　Praise Him the more,
Bacchanals, Cadmus-born;
　　　Praise with sore
Agony, yea, with tears!
Great are the gifts he bears!
Hands that a mother rears
　　　Red with gore!

Leader
But stay, Agâvê cometh!　And her eyes
Make fire around her, reeling!　Ho, the prize
Cometh!　All hail, O Rout of Dionyse!
[*Enter from the Mountain* Agave, *mad, and to all seeming
wondrously happy, bearing the head of* Pentheus *in her
hand.　The* Chorus Maidens *stand horror-struck at the
sight; the* Leader, *also horror-struck, strives to accept it
and rejoice in it as the God's deed.*

Agave
Ye from the lands of Morn!

Leader
Call me not; I give praise!

Agave
Lo, from the trunk new-shorn
Hither a Mountain Thorn
Bear we!　O Asia-born
　　　Bacchanals, bless this chase!

Leader
I see.　Yea; I see.
Have I not welcomed thee?

E

AGAVE (*very calmly and peacefully*)
He was young in the wildwood:
　Without nets I caught him!
　Nay; look without fear on
　　The Lion; I have ta'en him!

LEADER
Where in the wildwood?
　Whence have ye brought him?

AGAVE
Kithaeron. . . .

LEADER
　　　　Kithaeron?
AGAVE
The Mountain hath slain him!

LEADER
Who first came nigh him?

AGAVE
I, I, 'tis confessèd!
And they named me there by him
　Agâvê the Blessèd!

LEADER
Who was next in the band on him?

AGAVE
The daughters. . . .

LEADER
　　　　The daughters?

AGAVE

Of Cadmus laid hand on him.
    But the swift hand that slaughters
Is mine; mine is the praise!
Bless ye this day of days!

[*The* LEADER *tries to speak, but is not able;* AGAVE *begins gently stroking the head.*

AGAVE

Gather ye now to the feast!

LEADER

Feast!—O miserable!

AGAVE

See, it falls to his breast,
Curling and gently tressed,
The hair of the Wild Bull's crest—
    The young steer of the fell!

LEADER

Most like a beast of the wild
That head, those locks defiled.

AGAVE (*lifting up the head, more excitedly*)

He wakened his Mad Ones,
    A Chase-God, a wise God!
        He sprang them to seize this!
            He preys where his band preys.

LEADER (*brooding, with horror*)

In the trail of thy Mad Ones
    Thou tearest thy prize, God!

67

AGAVE
Dost praise it?

LEADER
I praise this?

AGAVE
Ah, soon shall the land praise!

LEADER
And Pentheus, O Mother
Thy child?

AGAVE
He shall cry on
My name as none other,
Bless the spoils of the Lion!

LEADER
Aye, strange is thy treasure!

AGAVE
And strange was the taking!

LEADER
Thou art glad?

AGAVE
Beyond measure;
Yea, glad in the breaking
Of dawn upon all this land,
By the prize, the prize of my hand!

LEADER

Show then to all the land, unhappy one,
The trophy of this deed that thou hast done!

AGAVE

Ho, all ye men that round the citadel
And shining towers of ancient Thêbê dwell,
Come!   Look upon this prize, this lion's spoil,
That we have taken—yea, with our own toil,
We, Cadmus' daughters!   Not with leathern-set
Thessalian javelins, not with hunter's net,
Only white arms and swift hands' bladed fall.
Why make ye much ado, and boast withal
Your armourers' engines?   See, these palms were bare
That caught the angry beast, and held, and tare
The limbs of him! . . . Father! . . . Go, bring to me
My father! . . . Aye, and Pentheus, where is he,
My son?   He shall set up a ladder-stair
Against this house, and in the triglyphs there
Nail me this lion's head, that gloriously
I bring ye, having slain him—I, even I!

[*She goes through the crowd towards the Castle, showing the
head and looking for a place to hang it.   Enter from the
Mountain* CADMUS, *with attendants, bearing the body of*
PENTHEUS *on a bier.*

CADMUS

On, with your awful burden.   Follow me,
Thralls, to his house, whose body grievously
With many a weary search at last in dim
Kithaeron's glens I found, torn limb from limb,
And through the interweaving forest weed
Scattered.—Men told me of my daughters' deed,

When I was just returned within these walls,
With grey Teiresias, from the Bacchanals.
And back I hied me to the hills again
To seek my murdered son. There saw I plain
Actaeon's mother, ranging where he died,
Autonoë; and Ino by her side,
Wandering ghastly in the pine-copses.

   Agâvê was not there. The rumour is
She cometh fleet-foot hither.—Ah! 'Tis true;
A sight I scarce can bend mine eyes unto.

AGAVE
(turning from the Palace and seeing him)

My father, a great boast is thine this hour.
Thou hast begotten daughters, high in power
And valiant above all mankind—yea, all
Valiant, though none like me! I have let fall
The shuttle by the loom, and raised my hand
For higher things, to slay from out thy land
Wild beasts! See, in mine arms I bear the prize,
That nailed above these portals it may rise
To show what things thy daughters did! Do thou
Take it, and call a feast. Proud art thou now
And highly favoured in our valiancy!

CADMUS

O depth of grief, how can I fathom thee
Or look upon thee!—Poor, poor, bloodstained hand!
Poor sisters!—A fair sacrifice to stand
Before God's altars, daughter; yea, and call
Me and my citizens to feast withal!

   Nay, let me weep—for thine affliction most,
Then for mine own. All, all of us are lost,
Not wrongfully, yet is it hard, from one
Who might have loved—our Bromios, our own!

AGAVE

How crabbèd and how scowling in the eyes
Is man's old age!—Would that my son likewise
Were happy of his hunting, in my way,
When with his warrior bands he will essay
The wild beast!—Nay, his valiance is to fight
With God's will!   Father, thou shouldst set him right. . . .
Will no one bring him hither, that mine eyes
May look on his, and show him this my prize!

CADMUS

Alas, if ever ye can know again
The truth of what ye did, what depth of pain
That truth shall bring!   Or were it best to wait
Darkened for evermore, and deem your state
Not misery, though ye know no happiness?

AGAVE

What seest thou here to chide, or not to bless?

CADMUS (*after hesitation, resolving himself*)
Raise me thine eyes to yon blue dome of air!

AGAVE

'Tis done.   What dost thou bid me seek for there?

CADMUS

Is it the same, or changèd in thy sight?

AGAVE

More shining than before, more heavenly bright!

CADMUS

And that wild tremor, is it with thee still?

AGAVE (*troubled*)

I know not what thou sayest; but my will
Clears, and some change cometh, I know not how.

CADMUS

Canst hearken then, being changed, and answer, now?

AGAVE

I have forgotten something; else I could.

CADMUS

What husband led thee of old from mine abode?

AGAVE

Echîon, whom men named the Child of Earth.

CADMUS

And what child in Echîon's house had birth?

AGAVE

Pentheus, of my love and his father's bred.

CADMUS

Thou bearest in thine arms an head—what head?

AGAVE

(*beginning to tremble, and not looking at what she carries*)
A lion's—so they all said in the chase.

CADMUS

Turn to it now—'tis no long toil—and gaze.

AGAVE

Ah! What is this? What am I carrying here?

CADMUS

Look once upon it full, till all be clear!

AGAVE

I see ... most deadly pain!   Oh, woe is me!

CADMUS

Wears it the likeness of a lion to thee?

AGAVE

No; 'tis the head—O God!—of Pentheus, this!

CADMUS

Blood-drenched ere thou wouldst know him!   Aye, 'tis his.

AGAVE

Who slew him?—How came I to hold this thing?

CADMUS

O cruel Truth, is this thine home-coming?

AGAVE

Answer!   My heart is hanging on thy breath!

CADMUS

'Twas thou.—Thou and thy sisters wrought his death.

AGAVE

In what place was it?   His own house, or where?

CADMUS

Where the dogs tore Actaeon, even there.

AGAVE

Why went he to Kithaeron?   What sought he?

CADMUS

To mock the God and thine own ecstasy.

AGAVE

But how should we be on the hills this day?

CADMUS

Being mad!   A spirit drove all the land that way.

AGAVE

'Tis Dionyse hath done it.   Now I see.

CADMUS

Ye wronged Him.   Ye denied his deity.

AGAVE (*turning from him*)

Show me the body of the son I love!

CADMUS (*leading her to the bier*)

'Tis here, my child.   Hard was the quest thereof.

AGAVE

Laid in due state?
[*As there is no answer, she lifts the veil of the bier and sees.*
                    Oh, if I wrought a sin,
'Twas mine!   What portion had my child therein?

CADMUS

He made him like to you, adoring not
The God; who therefore to one bane hath brought
You and this body, wrecking all our line,
And me.   Aye, no man-child was ever mine;
And now this first-fruit of the flesh of thee,
Sad woman, foully here and frightfully

Lies murdered! Whom the house looked up unto,
[*Kneeling by the body.*
O Child, my daughter's child! who heldest true
My castle walls; and to the folk a name
Of fear thou wast; and no man sought to shame
My grey beard, when they knew that thou wast there,
Else had they swift reward!—And now I fare
Forth in dishonour, outcast, I, the great
Cadmus, who sowed the seed-rows of this state
Of Thebes, and reaped the harvest wonderful.
O my belovèd, though thy heart is dull
In death, O still belovèd, and alway
Belovèd! Never more, then, shalt thou lay
Thine hand to this white beard, and speak to me
Thy " Mother's Father "; ask " Who wrongeth thee?
Who stints thine honour, or with malice stirs
Thine heart? Speak, and I smite thine injurers!"
But now—woe, woe, to me and thee also,
Woe to thy mother and her sisters, woe
Alway! Oh, whoso walketh not in dread
Of Gods, let him but look on this man dead!

LEADER

Lo, I weep with thee. 'Twas but due reward
God sent on Pentheus; but for thee . . . 'Tis hard.

AGAVE

My father, thou canst see the change in me,

   *   *   *   *   *
   *   *   *   *   *

[*A page or more has been here torn out of the MS. from which all our copies of " The Bacchae " are derived. It evidently contained a speech of Agâvê (followed presumably by some words of the Chorus), and an appearance of* DIONYSUS *upon a cloud. He must have pronounced judgment upon the Thebans in general, and especially upon the daughters of* CADMUS, *have justified his own action, and declared his determination to establish his godhead. Where the MS. begins again, we find him addressing* CADMUS.]

*   *   *   *   *

DIONYSUS

*   *   *   *   *
*   *   *   *   *

And tell of Time, what gifts for thee he bears,
What griefs and wonders in the winding years.
For thou must change and be a Serpent Thing
Strange, and beside thee she whom thou didst bring
Of old to be thy bride from Heaven afar,
Harmonia, daughter of the Lord of War.
Yea, and a chariot of kine—so spake
The word of Zeus—thee and thy Queen shall take
Through many lands, Lord of a wild array
Of orient spears.   And many towns shall they
Destroy beneath thee, that vast horde, until
They touch Apollo's dwelling, and fulfil
Their doom, back driven on stormy ways and steep.
Thee only and thy spouse shall Ares keep,
And save alive to the Islands of the Blest.
   Thus speaketh Dionysus, Son confessed
Of no man but of Zeus!—Ah, had ye seen
Truth in the hour ye would not, all had been
Well with ye, and the Child of God your friend!

AGAVE

Dionysus, we beseech thee.   We have sinned.

DIONYSUS

Too late!   When there was time, ye knew me not.

AGAVE

We have confessed.   Yet is thine hand too hot.

DIONYSUS

Ye mocked me, being God; this is your wage.

AGAVE

Should God be like a proud man in his rage?

DIONYSUS

'Tis as my sire, Zeus, willed it long ago.

AGAVE (*turning from him almost with disdain*)

Old Man, the word is spoken; we must go.

DIONYSUS

And seeing ye must, what is it that ye wait?

CADMUS

Child, we are come into a deadly strait,
All; thou, poor sufferer, and thy sisters twain,
And my sad self.   Far off to barbarous men,
A grey-haired wanderer, I must take my road.
And then the oracle, the doom of God,
That I must lead a raging horde far-flown
To prey on Hellas; lead my spouse, mine own
Harmonia, Ares' child, discorporate
And haunting forms, dragon and dragon-mate,
Against the tombs and altar-stones of Greece,
Lance upon lance behind us; and not cease
From toils, like other men, nor dream, nor past
The foam of Acheron find my peace at last.

AGAVE

Father!   And I must wander far from thee!

CADMUS

O Child, why wilt thou reach thine arms to me,
As yearns the milk-white swan, when old swans die?

AGAVE

Where shall I turn me else?   No home have I.

CADMUS

I know not; I can help thee not.

AGAVE

Farewell, O home, O ancient tower!
Lo, I am outcast from my bower,
And leave ye for a worser lot.

CADMUS

Go forth, go forth to misery,
The way Actaeon's father went!

AGAVE

Father, for thee my tears are spent.

CADMUS

Nay, Child, 'tis I must weep for thee;
For thee and for thy sisters twain.

AGAVE

On all this house, in bitter wise,
Our Lord and Master, Dionyse,
Hath poured the utter dregs of pain.

DIONYSUS

In bitter wise, for bitter was the shame
Ye did me, when Thebes honoured not my name.

AGAVE

Then lead me where my sisters be;
Together let our tears be shed,
Our ways be wandered; where no red
Kithaeron waits to gaze on me;
Nor I gaze back; no thyrsus stem,
Nor song, nor memory in the air.
Oh, other Bacchanals be there,
Not I, not I, to dream of them!

[AGAVE *with her group of attendants goes out on the side away
from the Mountain.* DIONYSUS *rises upon the Cloud and
disappears.*

CHORUS

There be many shapes of mystery.
And many things God makes to be,
Past hope or fear.
And the end men looked for cometh not,
And a path is there where no man thought.
So hath it fallen here.   [*Exeunt.*

79

NOTES ON THE BACCHAE

INTRODUCTORY NOTE

THE *Bacchae*, being from one point of view a religious drama, a kind of "mystery play," is highly traditional in form and substance, and repeats a canonical Dionysiac legend, often previously treated; for example, in the *Edoni* of Aeschylus. It is full of allusions both to the myth and to the religion of Dionysus.

1. The Myth, as implied by Euripides. Semelê, daughter of Cadmus, being loved by Zeus, asked her divine lover to appear to her once in his full glory; he came, a blaze of miraculous lightning, in the ecstasy of which Semelê died, giving premature birth to a son. Zeus, to save this child's life and make him truly God as well as Man, tore open his own flesh and therein fostered the child till in due time, by a miraculous and mysterious Second Birth, the child of Semelê came to full life as God.

2. The Religion of Dionysus is hard to formulate or even describe, both because of its composite origins and because of its condition of constant vitality, fluctuation, and development.

(*a*) The first datum, apparently, is the introduction from Thrace of the characteristic God of the wild northern mountains, a God of Intoxication, of Inspiration, a giver of superhuman or immortal life. His worship is superposed upon that of divers native Tree or Vegetation Gods, already worshipped in Greece. He becomes specially associated with the Vine. Originally a god of the common folk, despised and unauthorised, he is eventually so strong as to be adopted into the Olympian hierarchy as the " youngest " of the Gods, son of Zeus. His " Olympian " name, so to speak, is Dionysus, but in his worship he is addressed by numbers of names, more or less mystic and secret—Bromios, Bacchios or Baccheus, Iacchos, Eleuthereus, Zagreus, Sabazios, etc. Some of these may be the names of old spirits whom he has displaced; some are his own Thracian or Asiatic names. Together with his many names, he has many shapes, especially appearing as a Bull, the type of strength, and a Serpent, which sloughs its skin and renews its life.

(b) This religion, very primitive and barbarous, but possessing a strong hold over the emotions of the common people, was seized upon and transfigured by the great wave of religious reform, known under the name of Orphism, which swept over Greece and South Italy in the sixth century B.C., and influenced the teachings of such philosophers as Pythagoras, Aristeas, Empedocles, and the many writers on purification and the world after death. Orphism may very possibly represent an ancient Cretan religion in clash or fusion with one from Thrace. At any rate, it was grafted straight upon the Dionysus-worship, and, without rationalising, spiritualised and reformed it. Ascetic, mystical, ritualistic, and emotional, Orphism easily excited both enthusiasm and ridicule. It lent itself both to inspired saintliness and to imposture. In doctrine it laid especial stress upon sin and the sacerdotal purification of sin; on the eternal reward due beyond the grave to the pure and the impure, the pure living in an eternal ecstasy—"perpetual intoxication," as Plato satirically calls it—the impure toiling through long ages to wash out their stains. It recast in various ways the myth of Dionysus, and especially the story of his Second Birth. All true worshippers become in a mystical sense one with the God; they are born again and are "Bacchoi." Dionysus being the God within, the perfectly pure soul is possessed by the God wholly, and becomes nothing but the God.

Based on very primitive rites and feelings, on the religion of men who made their gods in the image of snakes and bulls and fawns, because they hardly felt any difference of kind between themselves and the animals, the worship of Dionysus kept always this feeling of kinship with wild things. The beautiful side of this feeling is vividly conspicuous in *The Bacchae*. And the horrible side is not in the least concealed.

A curious relic of primitive superstition and cruelty remained firmly imbedded in Orphism—a doctrine irrational and unintelligible, and for that very reason wrapped in the deepest and most sacred mystery: a belief in the sacrifice of Dionysus himself, and the purification of man by his blood.

In its agricultural form this rite was harmless enough. Dionysus was the grape and its juice his blood. Osiris was the wheat; the sowing of the grain meant the tearing (Sparagmos) and scattering of his body. But it seems that the savage Thracians, in the fury of their worship on the mountains, when they were possessed by the God and became "wild beasts," actually tore with their teeth and hands any hares, goats, fawns, or the like that they came across. There survives a constant tradition of inspired Bacchanals in their miraculous strength tearing even bulls asunder—a feat, happily, beyond the bounds of human possibility. The wild beast that tore was, of course, the savage God himself. And by one of those curious confusions of thought, which seem so inconceivable to us and so absolutely natural and obvious to primitive men, the beast torn was also the God. The mystic congregations of later times, in their most holy gatherings, solemnly partook of the blood of a bull, which was, by a mystery, the blood of Dionysus-Zagreus himself, the "Bull of God," slain in sacrifice for the purification of man. And the Maenads of poetry and myth, among more beautiful proofs of their superhuman or infra-human character, have always to tear the surrogate of their god in pieces and taste of his blood. It is noteworthy, and throws much light on the spirit of Orphism, that apart from this sacramental tasting of the blood, the Orphic worshipper held it an abomination to eat the flesh of animals at all. The same religious fervour and zeal for purity which made him reject the pollution of animal food, made him at the same time cling to a ceremonial which would utterly disgust the ordinary hardened flesh-eater. It fascinated him just because it was so incredibly primitive and uncanny; because it was a mystery which transcended reason.

It will be observed that Euripides, though certainly familiar with Orphism—which he mentions in *The Hippolytus* and treated at length in *The Cretans*—has in *The Bacchae* gone back behind Orphism to the more primitive stuff from which it was made. He has little reference to any specially Orphic doctrine; not a word, for instance, about the immortality of the soul. And his idealisation or spiritualisation of Dionysus-worship proceeds along the lines of his own thought, not on those already fixed by the Orphic teachers.

———

P. 8, l. 17, *Asia all, that by the salt sea lies*, etc., *i.e.* the coasts of Asia Minor inhabited by Greeks, Ionia, Aeolis, and Doris.

P. 8, l. 27, *From Dian seed.*—Dian = belonging to Zeus. The name Dionysus seemed to be derived from Διός, the genitive of "Zeus."

P. 9, l. 50, *Should this Theban town essay with wrath and battle*, etc.—This suggestion of a possibility which is never realised or approached is a method often used by the Greek poets for reconciling variant forms of a traditional story. There are traces of a version in which Pentheus led an army.

Pp. 10–14, ll. 64–169.—This first song of the Chorus covers a great deal of Bacchic doctrine and myth. The first strophe, " Oh blessèd he in all wise," etc., describes the bliss of Bacchic purity; the antistrophe gives the two births of Dionysus, from Semelê and from the body of Zeus, mentioning his mystic epiphanies as Bull and as Serpent. The next strophe is an appeal to Thebes, the birthplace or " nurse " of the God's mother, Semelê; the antistrophe, an appeal to the cavern in Crete, the birthplace of Zeus, the God's father, and the original home of the mystic Timbrel. The Epode, or closing song, is full, not of doctrine, but of the pure poetry of the worship.

Pp. 14–22, ll. 170–369, *Teiresias and Cadmus.*—Teiresias seems to be not a spokesman of the poet's own views—far from it—but a type of the more cultured sort of Dionysiac priest, not very enlightened, but ready to abate some of the extreme dogmas of his creed if he may keep the rest. Cadmus, quite a different character, takes a very human and earthly point of view: the God is probably a true God; but even if he is false, there is no great harm done, and the worship will bring renown to Thebes and the royal family. It is noteworthy how full of pity Cadmus is—the sympathetic kindliness of the sons of this world as contrasted with the pitilessness of gods and their devotees. See especially the last scenes of the play. Even his final outburst of despair at not dying like other men (p. 80), shows the same sympathetic humanity.

NOTES

Pp. 17 ff., ll. 215–262.—Pentheus, though his case against the new worship is so good, and he might so easily have been made into a fine martyr, like Hippolytus, is left harsh and unpleasant, and very close in type to the ordinary "tyrant" of Greek tragedy (cf. pp. 22, 46). It is also noteworthy, I think, that he is, as it were, out of tone with the other characters. He belongs to a different atmosphere, like, to take a recent instance, Golaud in *Pelléas et Mélisande*.

P. 18, l. 263, *Injurious King*, etc.—It is a mark of the highly traditional style of this play that it allows the Chorus Leader to make remarks which are not "asides," but are yet not heard or noticed by anybody.

P. 18, l. 264, *Sower of the Giants' Sod.*—Cadmus, by divine guidance, slew a dragon and sowed the teeth of it like seed in the "Field of Ares." From the teeth rose a harvest of Earth-born, or "Giant" warriors, of whom Echîon was one.

P. 19, l. 287, *Learn the truth of it, cleared from the false.* —This timid essay in rationalism reminds one of similar efforts in Pindar (e.g. *Ol.* i). It is the product of a religious and unspeculative mind, not feeling difficulties itself, but troubled by other people's questions and objections. (See above on Teiresias.)

P. 19, l. 292, *The world-encircling fire.*—This fire, or ether, was the ordinary material of which phantoms or apparitions were made.

Pp. 21–22, ll. 330–369.—These three speeches are very clearly contrasted. Cadmus, thoroughly human, thinking of sympathy and expediency, and vividly remembering the fate of his other grandson, Actaeon; Pentheus, angry and "tyrannical"; Teiresias speaking like a Christian priest of the Middle Ages, almost like Tennyson's Becket.

P. 22, l. 370.—The goddess Ὁσία, " Purity," seems to be one of the many abstractions which were half personified by philosophy and by Orphism. It is possible that the word is really adjectival, " Immaculate One," and originally an epithet of some more definite goddess, e.g. as Miss Harrison suggests, of Nemesis.

In this and other choruses it is very uncertain how the lines should be distributed between the whole chorus, the two semi-choruses, and the various individual choreutae.

P. 26, l. 453, *Marry, a fair shape.*—In Aeschylus' *Edoni* also Dionysus is of almost feminine beauty.

P. 27, l. 471, *These emblems.*—There were generally associated with mysteries, or special forms of worship, certain relics or sacred implements, without which the rites could not be performed. Cf. Hdt. vii. 153, where Telines of Gela stole the sacred implements or emblems of the nether gods, so that no worship could be performed, and the town was, as it were, excommunicated.

P. 30, ll. 493 ff., *The soldiers cut off the tress.*—The stage directions here are difficult. It is conceivable that none of Pentheus' threats are carried out at all; that the God mysteriously paralyses the hand that is lifted to take his rod without Pentheus himself knowing it. But I think it more likely that the humiliation of Dionysus is made, as far as externals go, complete, and that it is not till later that he begins to show his superhuman powers.

P. 31, l. 508, *So let it be.*—The name Pentheus suggests 'mourner,' from *penthos*, ' mourning.'

P. 32, l. 519, *Acheloüs' roaming daughter.*—Acheloüs was the Father of all Rivers.

P. 34, l. 556, *In thine own Nysa.*—An unknown divine

mountain, supposed to account for the second part of the name Dionysus.

P. 34, l. 571, *Cross the Lydias*, etc.—These are rivers of Thrace which Dionysus must cross in his passage from the East, the Lydias, the Axios, and some other, perhaps the Haliacmon, which is called "the father-stream of story."

P. 35, l. 579, *A Voice, a Voice.*—Bromios, the God of Many Voices—for, whatever the real derivation, the fifth-century Greeks certainly associated the name with βρέμω, 'to roar'—manifests himself as a voice here and below (p. 62).

Pp. 36–38, ll. 604–641, *Ye Damsels of the Morning Hills*, etc.—This scene in longer metre always strikes me as a little unlike the style of Euripides, and inferior. The earthquake and the accompanying incidents are part of the canonical legend and have to be brought in.   Cf. the *Edoni*.

P. 44, ll. 781 ff., *Call all that spur the charger*, etc.—The typical 'Ercles vein' of the tragic tyrant.

Pp. 46–50, ll. 810 ff.—This scene of the 'hypnotising' —if one may use the word—of Pentheus probably depends much on the action, which, however, I have not ventured to prescribe.   Pentheus seems to struggle against the process all through, to be amazed at himself for consenting, while constantly finding fresh reasons for doing so.

P. 48, l. 822, *Am I a woman, then.*—The robe and coif were, in the original legend, marks of the Thracian dress worn by the Thracian followers of Dionysus, and notably by Orpheus.   The tradition became fixed that Pentheus wore such a robe and coif; and to the Greeks of Euripides' time such a dress seemed to be a woman's.   Hence this turn of the story.

P. 51, ll. 877–881.—The refrain of this chorus about the fawn is difficult to interpret. I have practically interpolated the third line (" To stand from fear set free, to breathe and wait "), in order (1) to show the connection of ideas; (2) to make clearer the meaning (as I understand it) of the two Orphic formulæ, " What is beautiful is beloved for ever," and " A hand uplifted over the head of Hate." If I am wrong, the refrain is probably a mere cry for revenge, in the tone of the refrain, " Hither for doom and deed," on p. 58. It is one of the many passages where there is a sharp antagonism between the two spirits of the Chorus, first, as furious Bacchanals, and, secondly, as exponents of the idealised Bacchic religion of Euripides, which is so strongly expressed in the rest of this wonderful lyric.

P. 53, l. 920, *Is it a Wild Bull this?*—Pentheus, in his Bacchic possession, sees fitfully the mystic shapes of the God beneath the human disguise. This second-sight, the exaltation of spirit, and the feeling of supernatural strength come to Pentheus as they came to the two Old Men. But to them the change came peacefully and for good; to Pentheus it comes by force, stormily and for evil, because his will is against the God.

P. 57, l. 976, *O hounds raging and blind.*—i.e. Spirits of Madness. This lyric prepares us for what follows, especially for Agâvê's delusion, which otherwise might have been hard to understand. I have tried to keep the peculiar metre of the original, the dochmiac, with a few simple licences. The scheme is based on ◡́ ◡́◡́ or ◡́ ◡◡ ◡́◡́, the latter being much commoner.

Pp. 58–59, ll. 997–1011.—The greater part of this chorus is generally abandoned as unintelligible and corrupt. The last ten lines (" Knowledge, we are not foes," etc.) will, I think, make sense if we accept a very slight conjecture of my own. The four lines before that ("A strait pitiless mind," etc.) are an almost literal translation of the MS. reading, which, however, is incorrect in metre, and therefore cannot be exactly what Euripides wrote.

P. 60, l. 1036, *And deem'st thou Thebes so beggared.*— The couplet is incomplete in the MS. But the sense needed is obvious.

P. 63, l. 1120, *Let it not befall through sin of mine,* etc. —This note of unselfish feeling, of pity and humanity, becomes increasingly marked in all the victims of Dionysus towards the end of the play, and contrasts the more vividly with the God's pitilessness. Cadmus is always gentle, and always thinking of the sufferings of others; and, indeed, so is Agâvê, after her return to reason, though with more resentment against the oppressor.

Pp. 65–69, ll. 1165–1200.—This marvellous scene defies comment. But I may be excused for remarking (1) that the psychological change of the chorus is, to my mind, proved by the words of the original, and does not in the least depend on my interpolated stage directions; (2) the extraordinary exultation of Agâvê is part of her Bacchic possession. It is not to be supposed that, if she had really killed a lion, such joy would be the natural thing.

P. 67, *after* l. 1183, *The Leader tries to speak,* etc.—It is also possible that by some error of a scribe two lines have been omitted in the MS. But I think the explanation given in the text more probable and more dramatic.

P. 68, l. 1195, *And Pentheus, O Mother?*—The Leader mentions Pentheus, I suppose, in order deliberately to test Agâvê's delusion, to see if she is indeed utterly unconscious of the truth.

P. 71, l. 1267, *More shining than before*, etc.—The sight of the pure heaven brings back light to her mind—that is clear. But does she mean that the sky is brighter because of her madness which still remains, or that it is brighter now, after having been darkened in her madness?

P. 75, l. 1313, *And now I fare forth in dishonour*.—He has not yet been sentenced to exile, though he might well judge that after such pollution all his family would be banished.

P. 76, l. 1330, *For thou must change and be a Serpent Thing*, etc.—A prophecy like this is a very common occurrence in the last scenes of Euripides' tragedies. "The subject of the play is really a long chain of events. The poet fixes on some portion of it—the action of one day, generally speaking—and treats it as a piece of vivid concrete life, led up to by a merely narrative introduction (the Prologue), and melting away into a merely narrative close. The method is to our taste undramatic, but it is explicable enough. It falls in with the tendency of Greek art to finish, not with a climax, but with a lessening of strain " (*Greek Literature*, p. 267).

The prophecy was that Cadmus and Harmonia should be changed into serpents and should lead a host of barbarian invaders—identified with an Illyrian tribe, the Encheleis—against Hellas; they should prosper until they laid hands on the treasures of Delphi, and then be destroyed. Herodotus says that the Persians were influenced by this prophecy when they refrained from attacking Delphi (Hdt. ix. 42).